MW01453448

GRASSLANDS

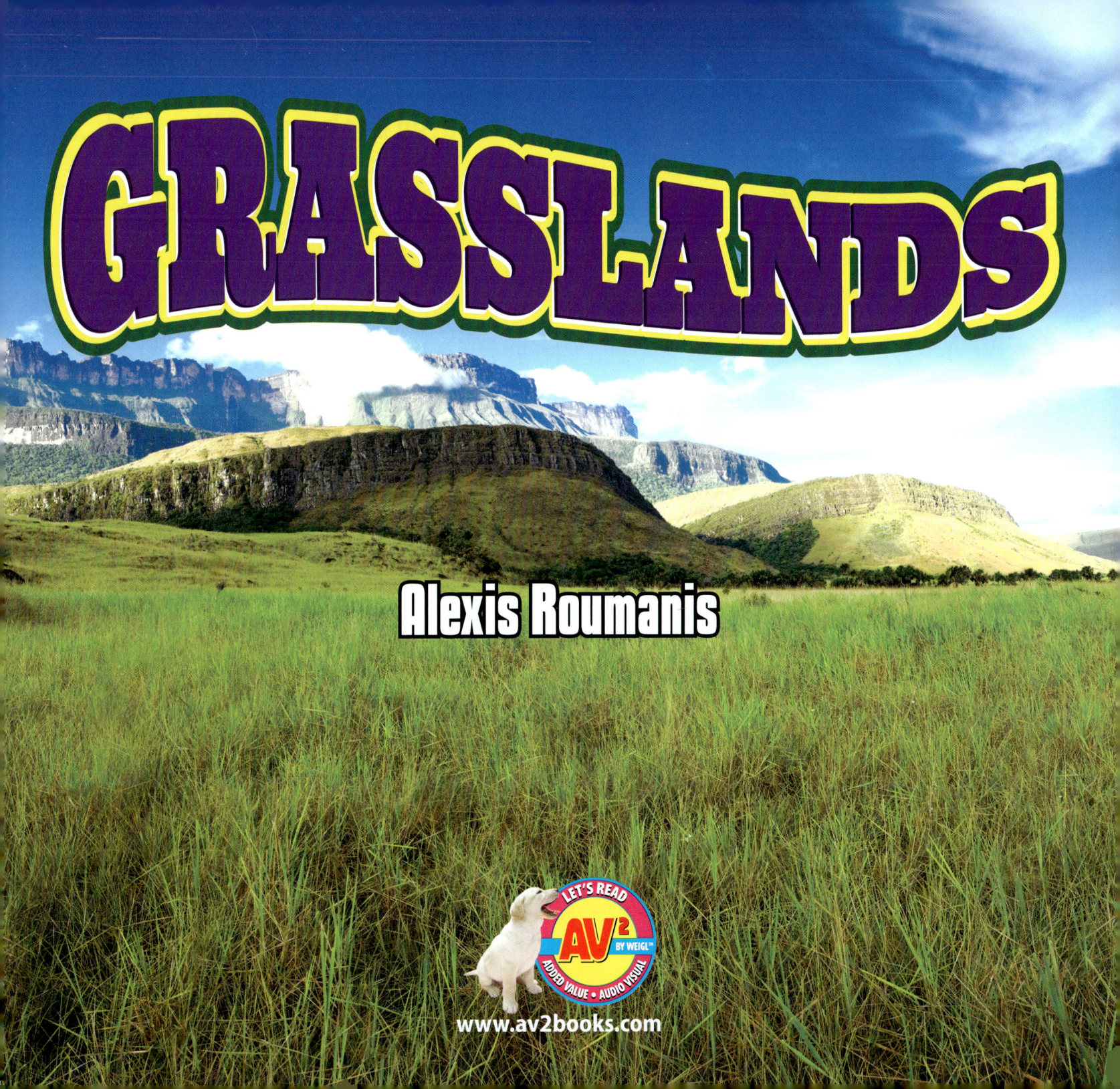

Alexis Roumanis

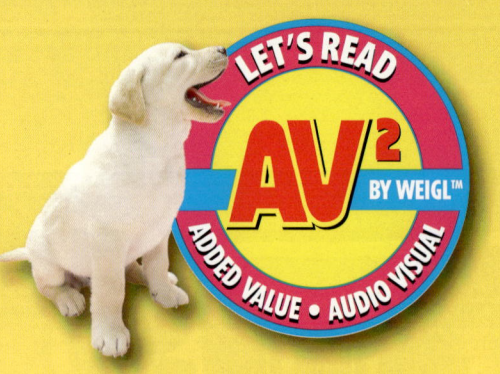

LET'S READ AV² BY WEIGL
ADDED VALUE · AUDIO VISUAL

AV² provides enriched content that supplements and complements this book. Weigl's AV² books strive to create inspired learning and engage young minds in a total learning experience.

Your AV² Media Enhanced books come alive with...

Audio
Listen to sections of the book read aloud.

Video
Watch informative video clips.

Embedded Weblinks
Gain additional information for research.

Try This!
Complete activities and hands-on experiments.

Key Words
Study vocabulary, and complete a matching word activity.

Quizzes
Test your knowledge.

Slide Show
View images and captions, and prepare a presentation.

... and much, much more!

Go to www.av2books.com, and enter this book's unique code.

BOOK CODE

X272824

AV² by Weigl brings you media enhanced books that support active learning.

Published by AV² by Weigl
350 5th Avenue, 59th Floor New York, NY 10118
Websites: www.av2books.com www.weigl.com

Copyright ©2016 AV² by Weigl
All rights reserved. No part of this publication may be reproduced, stored in a retrieval system, or transmitted in any form or by any means, electronic, mechanical, photocopying, recording, or otherwise, without the prior written permission of the publisher.

Library of Congress Cataloging-in-Publication Data

Roumanis, Alexis.
 Grasslands / Alexis Roumanis.
     pages cm. -- (Exploring Ecosystems)
 Includes index.
 ISBN 978-1-4896-3006-3 (hard cover : alk. paper) -- ISBN 978-1-4896-3007-0 (soft cover : alk. paper) --
 ISBN 978-1-4896-3008-7 (single user ebook) -- ISBN 978-1-4896-3009-4 (multi-user ebook)
 1. Grassland ecology--Juvenile literature. 2. Grasslands--Juvenile literature. I. Title.
 QH541.5.P7R58 2016
 577.4--dc23
                                            2014044094

Printed in the United States of America in Brainerd, Minnesota
1 2 3 4 5 6 7 8 9 0 19 18 17 16 15

012015
WEP051214

Project Coordinator: Jared Siemens
Design: Mandy Christiansen

Weigl acknowledges iStock and Getty Images as the primary image suppliers for this title.

GRASSLANDS

Contents

- 2 AV² Book Code
- 4 What Is a Grassland?
- 6 Where Are Grasslands?
- 8 Grassland Features
- 10 Grassland Ecosystem
- 12 Plant Life
- 14 Animal Life
- 16 On the Move
- 18 Human Activity
- 20 Saving the Grasslands
- 22 Grassland Quiz
- 24 Key Words

This is a grassland.
A grassland is a large piece of land where more grass grows than other plants.

5

6

A large part of Earth is grassland. Grasslands are often found in the center of large continents or near deserts.

The savannas in Africa are the largest tropical grasslands in the world.

Grasslands have deep soil that people use to grow crops and feed animals. Some grasslands have hot summers and cold winters. Others are hot all year.

Grasslands do not get enough rain for forests to grow.

9

Honeybees get food from flowers.

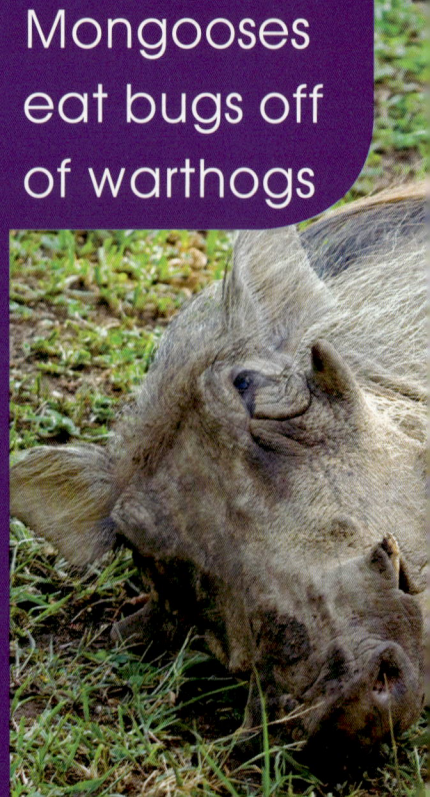

Ostriches and zebras work together to watch and listen for predators.

African oxpeckers help keep zebras clean.

Mongooses eat bugs off of warthogs

A grassland ecosystem is a place made up of animals and plants that need each other in order to live.

Stinging ants keep the leaves of the acacia tree safe from hungry giraffes.

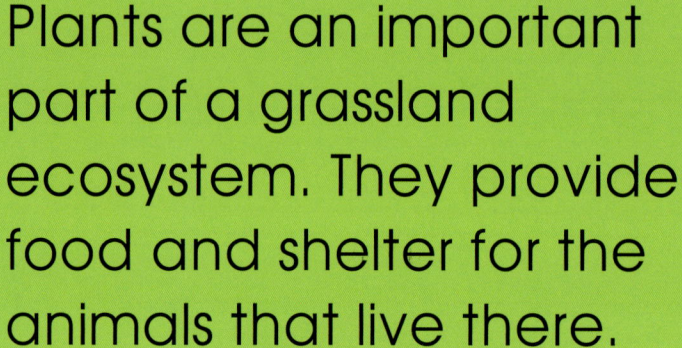

Plants are an important part of a grassland ecosystem. They provide food and shelter for the animals that live there.

Oat grass is an important crop in Australia.

Sunflowers can grow more than 10 feet (3 meters) high.

Wheat is grown on more land than any other kind of food plant.

Corn is part of the grass family.

Animals use acacia trees for shade from the Sun.

Elephants are the largest land animals in the world.

Burrowing owls can make a rattlesnake sound to scare away predators.

Female lions hunt in groups to catch large animals.

Zebras often live in grasslands in groups of up to 10,000.

Many different animals make their homes in grasslands.

Warthogs have special teeth made for grazing.

Animals often move from one place to another to find water and food. The largest movement of animals on Earth takes place on the Serengeti Plain of Africa.

Fires are nature's way of making grasslands new again.

17

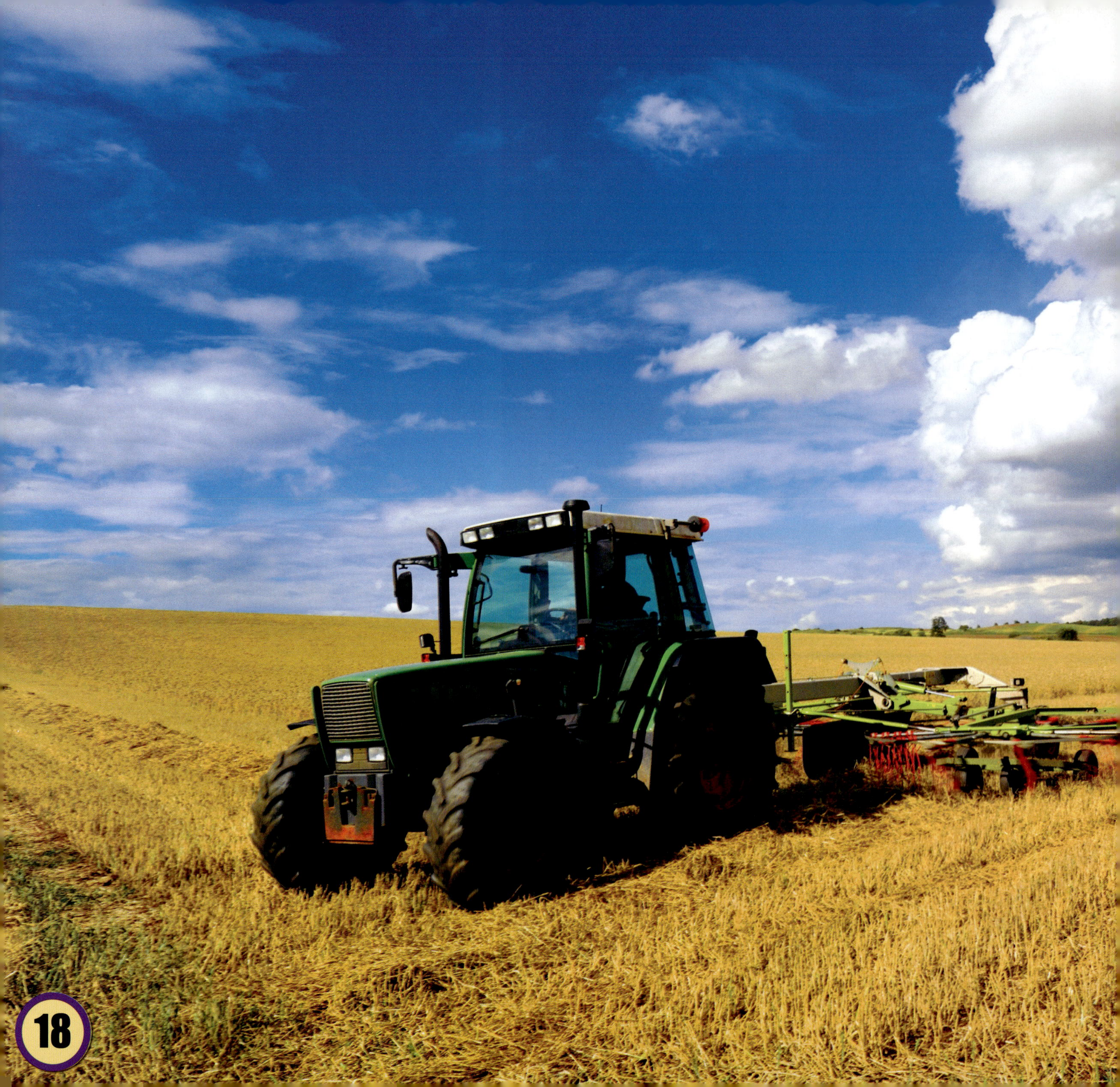

Most grasslands in North America are used for farming. Very little natural grasslands are left there today.

Animals have to find new homes when people use grasslands for houses and farms.

Farmers often plant grasses on old farmland. This helps make the grassland ready for animals to live there again.

People often help lost grassland animals to get back home.

21

Grassland Quiz

See what you have learned about grassland ecosystems.

Find these grassland animals and plants in the book. What are their names?

23

KEY WORDS

Research has shown that as much as 65 percent of all written material published in English is made up of 300 words. These 300 words cannot be taught using pictures or learned by sounding them out. They must be recognized by sight. This book contains 91 common sight words to help young readers improve their reading fluency and comprehension. This book also teaches young readers several important content words, such as proper nouns. These words are paired with pictures to aid in learning and improve understanding.

Page	Sight Words First Appearance
4	a, grows, is, land, large, more, of, other, plants, than, this, where
7	are, Earth, found, in, near, often, or, part, the, world
8	all, and, animals, do, enough, for, get, have, not, people, some, that, to, use, year
10	eat, food, from, help, keep, off, together, watch, work
11	each, leaves, live, made, need, place, tree, up
12	an, can, feet, high, important, there, they
13	any, family, kind, on
14	away, groups, make, sound
15	different, homes, many, their
16	again, another, find, move, new, one, takes, water, way
19	farms, houses, left, little, most, very, when
20	back, old

Page	Content Words First Appearance
4	grass, grassland, piece
7	center, continents, deserts, savannas
8	crops, forests, rain, soil, summers, winters
10	flowers, honeybees, mongooses, ostriches, oxpeckers, predators, warthogs, zebras
11	ants, ecosystem, giraffes
12	shelter, sunflowers
13	shade, Sun, wheat
14	elephants, lions, owls
15	teeth
16	Africa, fires, nature, Serengeti Plain
20	farmland

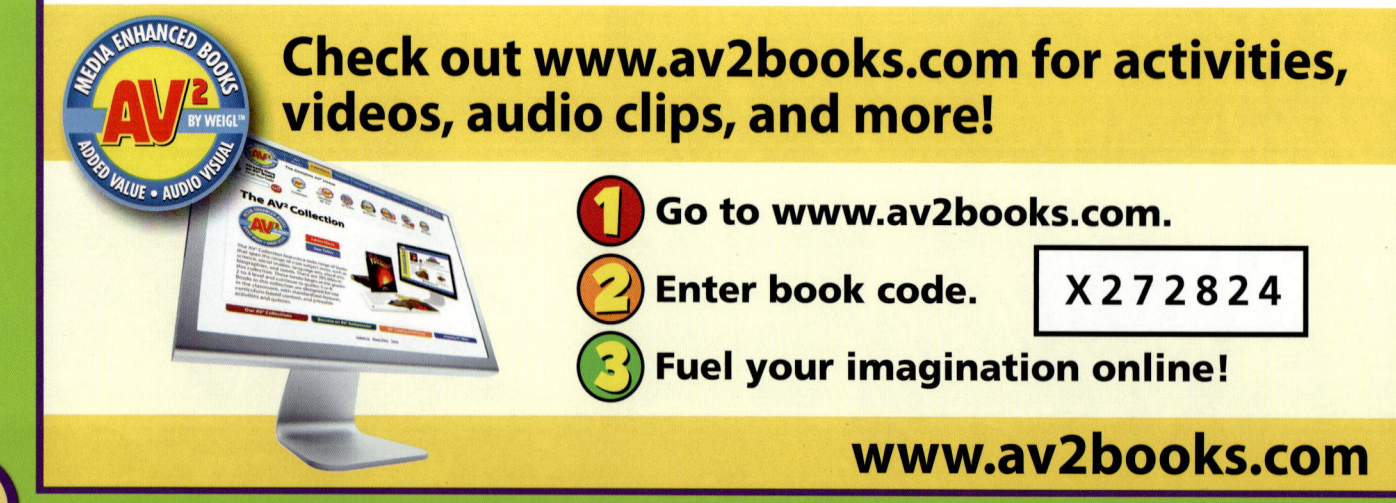

Check out www.av2books.com for activities, videos, audio clips, and more!

1. Go to www.av2books.com.
2. Enter book code. X272824
3. Fuel your imagination online!

www.av2books.com